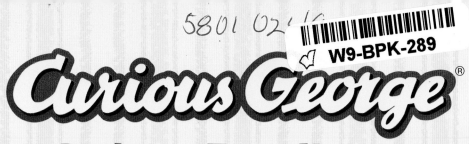

Curious George®

Builds a Tree House

Adaptation by Julie Tibbott
Based on the TV series teleplay written by Joe Fallon

Houghton Mifflin Harcourt
Boston   New York

ISBN: 978-0-544-86762-8 paper-over-board
ISBN: 978-0-544-86704-8 paperback

Design by Lauren Pettapiece
Cover art adaptation by Artful Doodlers Ltd.

www.hmhco.com
Printed in China
SCP 10 9 8 7 6 5 4 3 2 1
4500641636

AGES	GRADES	GUIDED READING LEVEL	READING RECOVERY LEVEL	LEXILE ® LEVEL
5–7	1	J	17	480L

George was a good little monkey, but sometimes he broke the house rules. Painting on the walls was against the rules.

So was buttering corn with your feet.
The animals outside didn't have to
worry about house rules.

That made it seem like a great place for
a monkey!
The tree was nice . . .

. . . until
it started raining.
George couldn't live in a tree and stay
dry—unless he had a tree house! Then he
could make his own house rules.

George went to see how other houses
were made.
Mrs. Renkins was building a chicken
coop. Maybe she could help.

George looked at
some drawings Mrs.
Renkins had.
"Those are my plans, George," she
explained. Of course! George needed a
plan. He drew a plan for his tree house.

Mrs. Renkins liked George's drawing.
"If you want to try building, take all
the wood you need," she said.

On the way home, George passed Mr. Quint, fixing the dock. "Hi, George," he said. "That's a lot of wood. You must be building something."

Mr. Quint offered George some nails.
"Take anything you need, neighbor!"

Armed with his Handy Monkey tool
set, George was ready to build.
This would be his house, and he would
make all the rules!

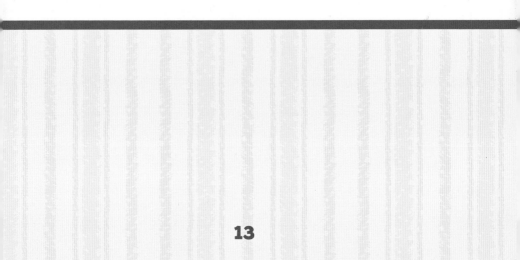

George chose
a piece of wood
for the floor of the tree house. He tried
to balance it on his favorite branch . . .
but it didn't stay up! Building was not
easy. How could he keep his floor from
tipping over?

Maybe he needed to balance his floor on two branches. Success!

Now it was time to put up the walls.
George remembered how Mr. Quint
used the tools on the dock. It was even
faster when you could use your feet!

After lots of hard work, there was only
one wall left to build.
But George was out of nails, and the
only piece of wood left was too big.

George went back to Mrs. Renkins's farm. She had told him he could have any wood he wanted.
Then he stopped at the dock for nails.

George's tree house was finally done! "Wow!" said the man with the yellow hat. "You built your own house. Where did you get all the wood and nails and . . ."

Just then, the neighbors showed up. "George! Did you take my wall?" asked Mrs. Renkins. Mr. Quint asked, "Did you take nails from my dock?"

George was sorry.
But then the neighbors saw his careful plans. They didn't want George to lose his tree house.

"It's okay. I did say you could have whatever nails you wanted," Mr. Quint said.
"And I can make a new wall," Mrs. Renkins said.

Now George had a place where he
made the rules. Rule #1: You have
to paint on the walls. And Rule #2:
Always butter corn with your feet!

What Are Houses Made Of?

Different kinds of houses use different kinds of building materials. Can you match the house to the material it was built with?

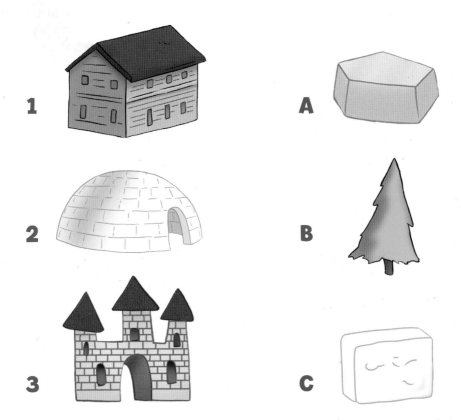

1

2

3

A

B

C

Make a Plan!

George learned that the first step in building something is making a plan. All you need is paper, something to draw with, and your imagination to make your own plans for a spectacular house! What will your house rules be?

Build a House with Sponge Blocks

Do you want to build things, just like George? You can make your own building blocks with ordinary household sponges!

You'll need . . .
Clean, dry sponges
Scissors

What to do:
Ask a grownup to help you cut the sponges into different shapes. Stack your sponge blocks together to build a house, a tower, or whatever else you can imagine!

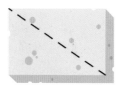

2 triangles

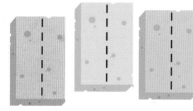

6 rectangles